T0063337

Her Smile, His Power

Sherrie Gourdin

WESTBOW°
PRESS
A DIVISION OF THOMAS NELSON
& ZONDERVAN

Scripture taken from the New King James Version.
Copyright © 1979, 1980, 1982 by Thomas Nelson,
Inc. Used by permission. All rights reserved.

WestBow Press books may be ordered through
booksellers or by contacting:

WestBow Press
A Division of Thomas Nelson & Zondervan
1663 Liberty Drive
Bloomington, IN 47403
www.westbowpress.com
1 (866) 928-1240

ISBN: 978-1-4908-6141-8 (sc)
ISBN: 978-1-4908-6142-5 (e)

Library of Congress Control Number: 2014921085

Printed in the United States of America.

WestBow Press rev. date: 12/11/2014

Contents

CHAPTER 1

Too Many Times

I was married when I was seventeen—almost eighteen—years old. I was looking for a way out of my parents' home. Sadly, this is the case for many young women if things at home are not what they should be.

Unfortunately, these marriages may end in separation and divorce because these young women didn't take the time they needed to find out what really makes a marriage work—they were too young to marry in the first place. This realization usually comes after they have had children. Now they are faced with the horror of divorce lawyers, trying to collecting child support, finding babysitters, and being both mom and dad, friend, counselor, nurse, cook, cleaning lady, healer of the heart, and on and on. They are forced to pick up this cross and carry it themselves. One day, they struggle to get out of bed only to look in the mirror and see someone else. "Who is that?" they ask. "That's not me. This is not what I planned for me. How could this be happening? What went wrong? Who is this reflection in my mirror, looking at me? Where's my prince? 'Someday my prince will come'—yeah, right."

These women will marry again, but this time they are middle-aged and have been listening to too many of her single friends, who say, "You better marry while you're still young enough to do it and while your kids are young. Nobody wants an old woman with older kids who are set in their ways." And again, they marry for the wrong reasons—except this time they have another man in their children's lives, and the children are not very fond of him.

This happened to me. I married for convenience and financial help. I was tired. No one understood me. Because I married at such a young age, that was all I knew. I thought that was all I could do.

But let me tell you—I can do so much more! And you can do so much more! You are the only one who has the power to change your course in life. If you are in a loveless marriage, do something about it, especially if your children don't like your husband. Your children will be with you to death, not him.

This is what I did—six months into my second marriage, I left. I was scared and insecure and had two children to feed and clothe and provide a safe roof over their heads. After living with a friend and working two jobs, I qualified for a mortgage. (The only thing worse than bad credit is no credit at all; I had none.) I started working with a Realtor, and she found a fixer-upper. With my parents' help, I bought my first home. Finally, I was on my own course and had my own home and time to myself.

I enjoyed the process of fixing up this cute little home with my daughter, who was then eighteen years old and the sweetest, most forgiving young woman ever. I knew I did not deserve her. I had put her through very hard times; she did not deserve that—no daughter should go through what I put her through. At that point, my son had moved out of state with his dad and wasn't speaking to me. Those were the darkest hours of my life. I had been too young to marry, but how do you beg forgiveness from your children for that? You can't. All you can do is love them.

Several years had gone by, and I was almost forty years old. One night I was out with a girlfriend, and I met *him*. Engraved on my mind and heart was, *Totally not going down that road ever again!* I had heard all the stories that said, "When the timing is right, you'll know when you meet him." What? I'd just *know*?

Well, he just wouldn't go away. He asked me to dance and followed me back to my table. He wanted my phone number. He was eleven years younger than I was, and women know that young men in a club want only one thing. I finally told him to go to the bar for a napkin to write my number on, and when he did, we left!

Some two weeks later, we were back at the same place. My girlfriend and I had been on a double date, and my date had burned a hole in my two-hundred-dollar outfit. I was so infuriated that I made our dates take us home, and I insisted that my date pay for my outfit that he'd ruined so carelessly. After that, my girlfriend wanted to go back to the place where I'd met *him* because she knew a guy who was having a party there. When we arrived there, *he* was there, waiting at the door. He'd been waiting there all night, because, he said, I'd never taken his number. With that, he took my cell phone and put his number in it.

A month later, I called him.

"It took you long enough," he said.

He was a man who recently had separated from his wife and was just out of the army after serving for six years. He drove a uniform truck for a living and gave all his money to his previous family, leaving very little for him to live on. He was working fifteen hours a day and spent every weekend with his child, which left very little time for me.

This man had nothing to offer but a little time and kindness, but he did all he could for me. He mowed the grass at my home, washed my car, and watched TV with me. He was the kindest man I had ever met.

It wasn't until he had the respect of my children that I thought something was there between us. It's one thing to win over small children, but when a man can earn the respect of adult children, that is something to notice.

He asked me to marry him after we'd been seeing each other for one month … and he patiently waited four years for my answer

This time, I married for love.

First, though, he had to prove to me that he wasn't going to change, that he was different from other men, and that not only would he love me unconditionally but my children as well.

When you take your time, no matter how long it takes, the truth always comes out.

His truth was unshakeable. He was a man of honor; he was trustworthy. I knew that if I placed my heart in his hands, he wouldn't crush it. He would nurture and lead by example.

It wasn't until after he had applied, passed the physical, had his interview, and was told when to report to the police academy that he told me he was going to be a policeman.

CHAPTER 2

Being a Helpmate

We saw each other for years, during which time he was being positive that I was the one, before I was comfortable with the idea of marriage again. I tried desperately to talk him out of it—even as we walked down the aisle, I whispered, "We do not have to do this. I'm not going anywhere."

He was sure. His confidence overcame my fear. This man was so kind and knew exactly what he wanted in life. He wasn't much of a talker. After being in the army for six years, he was emotionally detached—because he had to be. Transferring emotion in a marriage for a military person is very difficult. So I had many choices I had to make.

Everybody comes into a marriage with a past. How we choose to deal with the past affects our current situations. We need to pray and seek God's help always, make decisions unto the Lord, and choose wisely and carefully.

My situation seemed impossible. How could I compete with the past in his life? I truly needed God to intervene on my behalf.

When his child was young, we gave her a choice: when she was at our home, she had to be respectful and answer when we spoke to her, or she could not come over at all. I personally believe that a child under the age of eighteen does not have a choice, but I was raised in a different era. And in this case, I was not the biological parent. From that day on, there were no more visits to our home or sleepovers. He still saw her every weekend, but he picked her up, entertained her all day, and then returned her to her home. I had no contact with her at all.

This was where I had a lot of decisions to make. Something like this could have been handled wrong on my side and start the crumbling of a marriage, and even so, it stirred up a lot of anger in me. So for the thirteen years that he had visits with his daughter, I never said a word about it. I chose not to interfere in any way with his visitations. I never invited myself along or asked to be invited. And it was hurtful. He had to live three lives—one with me, one with his child, and one with his past. I could not make him choose me over family issues, and I knew this.

I'm a very outspoken and emotional person. The silence about this situation was very difficult for me. He never spoke of his past, so I never knew how many times he communicated with his daughter and ex-wife. I knew he did, though, and it was hurtful and a constant feeling that I did not count. I wasn't a part of the decision making at all. It gave me a strong sense on unimportance, especially when it came to how much money he gave them—if they needed extra, he just gave it to them. I was never asked about anything.

I had chosen to be a helpmate and to remain silent and trust that God knew what he was doing, because my husband was good to me. I did all I could for him all the time. I cooked every day when he came home, did his laundry, cleaned up after him, and waited on him continuously. I did all I could every day to make his life as easy as possible. I became a servant, but this was my choice. My mother had been an actual servant, and I had watched her serve, and it changed lives. I knew God was faithful; he is the only one who never lets you down. He never let my mother down, and I knew my choices would not be in vain and that they would bring forth life for us.

We are the choices that we make. I wanted a life with this man and was willing to lay the groundwork. I was willing to be a servant and not ask questions. I wanted a life with him.

CHAPTER 3

Getting Behind

I believe that a woman has the power to make or break a man. A woman can build or tear down a man anytime she wants. I do not believe, however, that anyone should hold such power over any one person.

I know that if I would have chosen to interfere, argue, or complain about the things that I knew in my heart were unjust and unfair to me, it would have been my downfall. Instead, I chose to pray for my husband daily. Every day, I asked God to bless him, show him favor, protect him because he was a policeman, give him wisdom, make him a great leader, and be respected by all who worked with him. I also prayed that all the choices he made would be the right ones for all who worked under him, I ask God to bless him financially and to keep him safe daily. I asked that he would be a great man, father, and husband and that everyone and everything around him and everything he touched would be blessed because of his presence.

I covered him with safety in prayers because he patrolled for seven years in the worst part of the city. He actually came home one day with a bullet hole in his car. At the end of his shift as a patrolman, he would meet in a designated area and turn in his paperwork. He worked in the projects, and people would drive by and shoot at officers. What makes a man want to put his life on the line for another person and for someone he does not know—complete strangers? I thought the very least I should do was pray for him.

It wasn't long before he started moving up in the ranks at his job and commanded his own precinct. All the while that he progressed in his job, I was on my knees, praying and asking God for favor. I kept quiet, did all I could for him, and was a support system. I saw my faithfulness rewarded through my husband.

I never complained about the hours he put in or the constant phone calls, extra duties, and everything else the job demanded of him. What the job didn't take from him, his ex-wife and daughter did. There wasn't much left after that.

I guess that constantly dealing with so many under his care and dealing with his ex-wife and daughter caused him to become even more quiet—it was like he was talked out and did not speak much at home.

Women do not like to share their husbands, but I had to share mine with the world. Being in the background, doing battle—that was my job, and I had to be good at it, as he was elevated through his job. This was tough. My life was put on hold ... but as a mother, I was used to that, and I understood.

I don't believe that I could have done what he had to do. He was a better person than I was.

I made a decision that I would get behind my husband and do all I could for him with prayer and action. When we do that as women, God not only blesses our husbands but he blesses us as well. You know what they say: "Behind every successful man is a woman ... on her knees"—or is that, "rolling her eyes"?

My husband was—and is—in control of so much. Not only is he responsible for all of the officers under him and their safety, but he also is in control of over an eighty-six-mile radius of the general public. Some people have coworkers at their jobs that they would rather not deal with every day. Well those little pains in the butt are nothing when compared to the criminals that my husband has to deal with on a daily basis. He deals with people that we wouldn't even want to know or ever see or meet. I would not want that crown. I had a hard enough time keeping my kids in line. It is much easier for me to walk behind my husband, in his shadow, than try to be ahead of him.

Try walking behind, and let your husband deal with the crap that could take you down. You most likely don't want to deal with it anyway. Your life will be much easier—I know mine was.

CHAPTER 4

Can He Be All He Needs to Be?

When we women marry, we have to let our husbands be in charge of us as the head of the house. "When a person turns to the Lord, God lifts the veil from his eyes" (2 Corinthians 3:16). The Bible also tells us, "Now the Lord is that Spirit: and where the Spirit of the Lord is, there is liberty" (2 Corinthians 3:17). The word *liberty* here means "no longer a slave; exempt from liability; free, unchained." This describes the freedom that comes with having our eyes opened. Suddenly, we see things in a new light. Only the Holy Spirit can break down our lifelong stubborn ways of seeing things, turn us around, and set us on a true course.

As I trusted God, the veil was removed from my husband's eyes. He began to see me differently. I became someone of importance—not that I wasn't important already, but I did not feel important enough. God showed me through my husband that I was important to my husband. Through my faithfulness of being a servant, he was becoming the husband I needed. I'm not saying that my husband was not a good husband, but he just was emotionally detached. Eventually, he became someone who showed he was attached to me.

Women want men like the men in movies—someone who is perfect. This is not reality. Perfect love casts out all fear. Perfect love is unconditional. It forgives all, covers all our mistakes, and heals our deepest wounds. By my obedience to my husband, he was able to become all he needed to be for the department and for me. If I had been a wife who complained or argued that he was never home and fought against him, he would have been crippled by my interference and his career would have been crippled as well—and it definitely would have caused war in our home. Nothing good ever comes of war; with war, there is suffering and death. I didn't want any part of that! I already had two dead marriages under my belt and was determined to succeed at this one, no matter the cost. I was too old to start over again and too tired to try.

By my obedience to God, by my being a servant to my husband and being a helpmate instead of a hindrance, my husband had the freedom to be all that he was to be for everyone.

So many times I have heard of women who forced their husbands choose between them and the job, or between them and the ex or the other children. I did not make my husband choose. Women who do so might as well put a gun to their heads; it will not end well. Men are headlines; women are the fine print, All he knows is that he has to work, has to eat, has to be a father, and has to be a husband—and this did not come with a manual.

So I had to be the type of person to help him through my submission, faithfulness, kindness, and patience, so that he could become all he could be as a man. Will you let your husband do that? Can you?

Find your liberty, unchain him, and set him free, so he can be all he needs to be, and you will be free.

CHAPTER 5

The Better He Is, the Better Off You Are

You will never receive deliverance unless you change. Your life and your situation will worsen. Stop building your case, pointing your finger, and justifying yourself. God will not meet you until you admit, "Nothing is going to change for me unless I'm changed."

How many more experts, counselors, or fruitless strivings must you endure before you wake up to the truth? If any healing or restoration is going to take place, you must take responsibility. Your miracle is dependent on your being changed.

I changed—in the sense that I know I cannot change a man. How many women marry with the thought that they will change their husbands? Too many. If you are not willing to change for the better, however, how in the world can he? If and when you are willing to change your ways, start simply—for example, by not saying anything when something rubs you the wrong way or you disagree with him. Small steps lead to a walk, which leads to a run. Pretty soon, you will find yourself not saying or doing negative things.

Of course, sometimes I thought, because I already have raised two children, that my way was best. I noticed every fault my husband had as a parent; therefore, I thought I was superior. Imagine that!

The woman's deliverance is real and lasting. With even the smallest beginning, faith starts to rise up in our hearts. We realize that God did it last week, and He can do it again this week. And he will. As my husband became a better, much stronger man at work and at home. I became a better person as well. Because of his strength, I became a woman who is a better wife, mother, homemaker, and friend. I became able to deal with tragic adversities in my life that otherwise might have put me in the grave.

Because I learned to place my life in this man's hands and trust that he knew best, he grew stronger and stronger, year after year. He grew in power at his job, with great respect, honor, and trust, and the men who worked for him praised him. No one ever said an unkind thing about him—not ever. Even my children sang his praises.

There is great power in your smile of silence. I was the better person, because he was better through prayer and example than through the cutting edge of my tongue. The better he became as a person, the better off I was. He makes me want to be a better woman. Can you see the power in that? Is anything stronger than a woman's will? Yes, there is God's will for us to be in perfect love through him.

When I became a better woman, the appearance of my face changed, and my mind was more positive. I got my weight in check, and the better I looked, the better I felt. The confidence that comes with control through him or by you is amazing. It was as if the weight of the cross I had carried for more than thirty years was lifted. Suddenly, I didn't have to be in charge—I didn't want to be, believe me. Anyone who has been a single parent will tell you that. But being in charge was all we knew, and nobody was going to tell us any different. Why did I ever want to wear the pants? God never intended for a woman to carry the load when he gave her help, such as a husband

The peace that comes with trust is immeasurable. Put your trust in God. He is much more equipped to handle your husband and you than you are. He knows what he is doing, but we sure don't—and that's a tough one to admit. So remember, the better your husband becomes, either at work or at home, the better you will be mentally and physically—I sleep soundly.

"A wife of noble charter is her husband's crown, but a disgraceful wife is like decay in his bones" (Proverbs 12:4). If you really think about that, how could we ever justify in our hearts arguing with our husbands and being disrespectful, whether in private or public? Show respect. Do yourself that favor. Hurting him only hurts you.

"Wives, submit to your husbands, as is fitting in the Lord. Husbands, love your wives and do not be harsh with them" (Colossians 3:18–19). This is a hard one. My heart goes out to the woman who has to bear this. Trust, and God will take away his harshness when you submit.

What do you have to lose if you try this? God is true to his word.

CHAPTER 6

Shut Up

I apologize for the title of this chapter, but there is simply no other way to put it. Do you agree that children and adults only know and gather their opinions based on what they hear you say and see you do? This includes your actions and reactions to people or your spouse. In my case, people are very close to me who are Christians, and they truly love God. They are real prayer warriors and are willing to pray and do battle with you any time you call on them. I have watched them for more than fifty years, and the one thing I have learned is that if I speak negatively about my husband or anyone, that is all someone knows about that person.

If your husband is not fully up to God's potential yet, it is easy to point out the negative in him. Speaking negatively isn't always done in a cruel way; it can be just talking about something that happened. For example, if you're having a problem and you discuss it innocently with a close family member, it's easy for that family member to form an opinion, simply based on what is coming from your mouth. You only get one chance to make a first impression. Life or death is in the power of the tongue. We are forgiven, not perfect. And because the family member loves you, the person you're talking about gets hung on the cross of judgment for life. Then that judgment spreads to everyone the family member knows, and suddenly, all the negativity is out there, floating around the universe. Constantly tearing down this one person, who God is trying to make better, becomes the topic of conversation every time the person's name is brought up. I hear it when I ask, "How is _____?" And that conversation starts with a sigh, a negative word, or a facial gesture.

Well, this wasn't going to happen to my husband. There are enough husbands hanging on that cross around the world, and mine wasn't going to be one of them. Regardless of what was going on in my home, I chose my words carefully and decided that every time someone mentioned my husband's name, it would be in praise. I will never forget the day my father said to me, "I finally have a son-in-law I can be proud of!" I had never heard my dad say that about anyone in my family, especially the men in my family.

After the honeymoon was over and we were back to regular life, I learned immediately that this man I had just married for love was different. He had a very difficult childhood—his father died when he was twelve years old, and his mother moved to across country, taking his brother and leaving him alone, With nobody's help at all, he raised himself and went to college for four years on a basketball scholarship. Everything he accomplished was on his own.

He was self-made and self-accomplished and had experienced abandonment that I could never understand. Because of this, things would be his way from that point on—no negotiating, ever. He was not a compassionate man—empathy and sympathy did not come naturally—and although he had a bachelor's degree in mass communication, communicating one-on-one with me just didn't happen. I had been married and had observed my family's marriages, and I was used to everything being shared, like money and problems. The women usually had control of the finances. They discussed certain subjects, sometimes to death, and the women would make their husbands see things their way eventually—or get what they wanted through arguing. I was used to yelling in a relationship, but not him—not ever. There was no arguing with him at all.

He interpreted arguing and disagreeing as my being displeased with him and suggested that I needed to move. "If you're not happy the way I do things, we should separate," he would say. "Then you can find someone you are happy with." How was I supposed to live with a man and never voice my opinion? I knew when this happened the very first time that if I wanted to have a life with him, I had to shut up and let him be in total charge of me and our house.

This was the most difficult thing I ever had to do. He earned the money, and if I needed anything, I had to ask for it. He would give me only the exact amount needed. I had no control of anything at all. I had to be quiet and trust him. I did not have a choice if I wanted to be with him. I had never known anyone like him. He never said one bad word about anyone and never voiced an opinion, even when asked. He had no prejudice. He was not prideful. He was hardworking—if he did not get a perfect score on a test, he considered that he'd failed. Everything he did had to be perfect, and he was the most focused, faithful man I had ever met. Only now do I realize he knew exactly what he was doing. God had got hold of that twelve-year-old boy and made him the strongest man in spirit, mentally, and physically. He accomplished and overcame a man's worst fears.

And he needed a wife who would walk his way, not hers. So I did. Because of this, he has been so favored by God that he has accomplished more in his life than any ten men. I believe that if I had not walked the very thin line of silence and obedience, he would just be another divorced man and would not have reached his level of power in the home, community, and his job today. He is greatly respected by all.

Because of my silence, God has changed this man to be all I need him to be in a husband. He is wonderful to me.

CHAPTER 7

Respect When He Doesn't Deserve It

I'm embarrassed by how many times I have thought that my husband didn't deserve my respect. Our husbands always deserve our respect, even when we think they don't. My husband was emotionally detached and quiet, but he also was kind, never raised his voice to me, and was very generous and kind to my children. He was the strong, silent type.

He was always there when I needed him. Maybe you think that a man like that surely deserves respect. Maybe you wish your own husband was like that. Even though my husband was all those things and more, he was very set in his ways—I think we all are, especially when we marry late in life.

He was a guy who would give freely and without question to his family. It seemed that anyone could ask for an amount of money and not give any explanation for it. Or he would ask in conversation, "Do you need any money?" He would check on them, and I'm glad he was that way—it shows character, kindness, and generosity. But when it came to me, I usually wasn't asked at random if I needed money. Even when I would say, "I'm broke. I don't have a dime," and I would ask for some money, he would ask, "What for?" Then again, I would feel like I wasn't important enough to him because he made me give an explanation. There was nothing wrong with his asking "What for?"—it made me accountable—but why didn't he ask others that question? They never had to give an explanation

He was a peacemaker. He never wanted to rock the boat or make waves with anyone, especially his family. But wait—*I* was family. Why did he ask me why I needed money? It wasn't until years and years later that I understood this, although to this day, I still feel it isn't fair. It's just his way. He thought I was important enough to marry and to take care of for the rest of his life—he provides everything for me. So when I asked for more that he'd already given, he needed an explanation. That's all; nothing more, nothing less, and don't read anything into it.

Another issue I had with him was not being informed. He never included me in decisions he made, whether important ones or the smallest thing. I found myself with feelings of resentment because he didn't include me in the decision making, especially when it came to how much money he gave to his family. I would try to offer my opinion, but it was not accepted, and he did not want to hear it. Because of that issue, it was hard at times to show respect, but I always did; he just never knew how I felt. I would do battle in my mind. I would dwell on him in my head, and it kept me up at night. What a fool I was to cause all that torment in my mind for nothing all those years! Just the simplest thing, such as having dinner ready, became an act of obedience to God, because I didn't want to do it for him—I'm ashamed to say that.

As wives, we think we need to know all—all he's thinking, doing, giving, and what he's going to do—but we don't need to know. My husband was plain and simple, just doing what a husband is supposed to do—being the man. His thought was, *Why burden her with all this trivia? She can't pay it or do it anyway,* He was a need-to-know man, and I didn't need to know all that … but I just wanted to know. He wasn't disrespecting me; he was just handling his business, as so many wives complain that their husbands don't do. He was doing his job as a man, a provider, and a husband, father, and friend. I'd previously had a husband who would not handle his business, and I had to be in charge of all the household affairs and money. I was not accustomed to someone who knew how to handle everything and was good at it.

Women often are forced to take charge. Their lives are a constant struggle, full of disappointments and broken hearts. Trusting someone to handle things is extremely difficult, especially for women who have had a lifetime of men who have let them down. I encourage you, however, to just let him do it. Life is so much easier when God makes you understand why—and he will.

Give up the burden. God gave me a husband to do what I wasn't called to do. I know this now, but I had to walk it first.

CHAPTER 8

In the Shadow in Public Places

My husband had grown to be such an important public figure in his career that everything in his life was under a microscope. His bosses, coworkers, and anyone else who was influential in the city or community watched him carefully. He did not get to his position by having chaos in his private life. His affairs had to be in order, and just as important, they had to appear to be in order in public. People watched all the time. So whenever I was with him in public, I was very respectful (which is not to say that I wasn't at home). I always praised him, was edifying, smiled a lot, and built him up to others. People talk, and they talk all the time. They do notice.

Even when it was something as simple as going to the movies, I walked one step behind him, unless he was holding my hand. Sloppy public displays of affection did not happen—I'm appalled when I see others is such displays; it is embarrassing to me and should not happen. I'm actually glad we did not do that. When we were out at a function where his coworkers would be, I always gave him the freedom to do what he needed to do—mingle, say hello, shake hands, talk, whatever it was. Many times we would go to a banquet, a dinner, or an opening, and as soon as we walked in, I was alone. I kept to myself, saying the hellos and introducing myself as the commander's wife. (If I said my name, nobody knew who I was, but they all knew him.) It was always his hour in the spotlight, but I knew it was important for me to be there, if only to show my support. There were times when I eventually would walk up to him and just stand there quietly, never getting an introduction to the people to whom he was speaking, but that was okay. It wasn't about me. A lot of wives would have a problem with this; they would be selfish and want the spotlight too. That only makes them look like immature babies. Self-confidence is much more attractive. My being the center of attention would have been embarrassing for him and annoying for everyone—and it would have been the last function to which he would have taken me. Then the ripple effect would have occurred. It would have appeared that he was not in control. How could anyone trust this man to be a leader of the city if he could not control his wife? Without my support, cooperation, and respect, it would have ruined his career and his being a leader in the eyes of the public. Women have the power to make or break a man.

When you are with your husband out in public, regardless of whether he is an important public figure, you do not need to be in the spotlight. Your being in his shadow will elevate you automatically; you will be noticed and respected, and the next time, people will remember your name as well. They will think of you fondly, and he will be respected more.

Now when my husband and I walk in a room, people come up to me, smile, and say hello to me.

CHAPTER 9

Support System

While my husband's life was being elevated by God, mine was falling apart. He was becoming accomplished and solid in his career; his life was falling into all the right places. It seemed that God was favoring him so much that God forgot about me.

I was diagnosed with arthritis of the spine and was having a lot of pain. I was constantly going to doctors and physical therapists and was living on painkillers. When I finally went to a spinal doctor, he decided to burn the nerves in my spine to relieve the pain—without that treatment, he said, I was headed for a wheelchair at the age of fifty.

Something as simple as walking was almost impossible for me. After four nerve studies, with a minimum of forty-eight needles in each leg and arm, there then were CAT scans, MRIs, ultrasounds, and many other tests. I now get four nerves burned in my back four times a year, which helps me to live without pain.

If that wasn't bad enough, the love of my life, my daughter, told me she was moving across country. I will never forget the day my darling daughter drove off down the street in that big truck packed with her entire life. I thought that this would kill me. My heart was so broken that I thought it was truly impossible to be comforted. I was depressed in such a way that nothing made me smile for a long time. I actually went on antidepressants, but they didn't help. Nothing helped. She left to live her life the way she wanted and where she wanted to live it. Any mother whose child has moved out of state can understand this pain. I knew that if she married and had children that I would be the grandma who only comes to visit once in a while. I'm the type of person who needs her children in her life every day. I never wanted them to leave at all. How do you stop being a mom?

Worrying about this beautiful woman living in the strange, huge city of Los Angeles was terrifying to me. What if something happened to her? It was a four-hour plane ride to LA. How could I get there fast enough? This crushed me.

And then I found out one month later that my son was moving out of state also. I felt that doom and disaster were upon me. My children were gone, my husband worked all the time, my family was out of state, and I was alone ... all the time.

My son's move to Florida was due to his job. This was an eight-hour drive. I helped him pack, said good-bye, and watched another child leave. This was more than I could bear. I felt that God was removing all that I loved from me, and I was alone. I found myself walking around our big house after my husband went to work, trying to do household chores and crying all the time. Time went by slowly.

After four years, my son moved back home. He lived with us. It was then that God unveiled a truth about my son. He was in trouble. He had been living a life that would have led to death if God had not intervened quickly. So I began to pray all the time about this. God was faithful and healed my son through divine deliverance. My husband was nonjudgmental, forgiving, and kind. He had unconditional love for my children, and his strength saw me through, with God's hand on me. I received peace when that should have been impossible.

While all this was going on I wanted to crawl under the covers and never come out. I certainly did not want to get up every day and act as if everything was okay, but my husband needed me. He had to be fed, his laundry had to be done, and he had an important job to do every day. I put on a fake smile; I didn't want to live. Why would God do this to me? What had I done? I thought this was my punishment for hurting my children through divorce. I had crippled their lives, and I deserved death. I now know that God had to get me totally alone and face down to bring me back up. I had to hit rock bottom. This was the time my husband needed to go from emotionally detached to attached. Inside, I was falling apart because I had no control over anything that was happening around me.

God showed me just how important I was to my husband, and my husband became more compassionate with me, showing sorrow for my situation. This, coming from a man who showed no emotion in most things, was huge. He was a rock for everyone, and he had to be. This gentle giant was gentle with me. I remained supportive and cared for him so much that my love was overwhelming for him.

No matter what the circumstances are in our lives, if we put the needs of others first, our needs will be met by the only one who can heal and deliver us out of the pit—our gracious Lord and Father, God.

CHAPTER 10

Favor from God

The only real failure is the failure to try. The measure of success is how we cope with disappointment, as we always must. We have tried in our different ways. Can I be blamed for feeling I am too old to change? Too scared of disappointment to start all over again? I get up in the morning, and I do my best—nothing else matters. But it's also true that the person who risks nothing does nothing and has nothing. Perhaps what we fear is that it might be the same. So I celebrate change, because as someone once said, everything will be all right in the end, and if it's not, then it's not quite the end!

It's hard enough to trust our husbands—men we see in the physical—but when we trust an unseen God, he shows us favor because of our trust and faith.

For years, when I prayed, I would ask God to show favor to my daughter, son, and husband at their jobs, with their employers, in relationships, and in their health and finances. I constantly covered them in showers of prayers. What kind of a mother would I be if I didn't do that? Wasn't it my job to pray for protection over my family? I had two children who were out of state and a cop for a husband; they needed covering. God was always faithful and did what I asked. I've heard that when we pray for others, God always listens. Little did I know that he would show me much favor down the road.

My husband is a very independent man. I'm someone who is very dependent, and I depended on my husband more than he needed me—that's for sure. After six years in the army, sometimes living in just a tent, he knew how to take care of himself. He could do laundry, sew his clothes, iron them, make a bed, and clean up after himself. I often found him sitting on the couch, sewing a hole in his uniform, and he never bothered me with it. Sometimes I wondered why I was here—the man was self-sufficient. It was this way for years.

Then small changes started happening to me. I noticed that he would come over to the couch where I was watching TV and for no reason, he'd reach down and kiss me, and hug me, and smile and look at me. If I commented on something I saw or would like to have, days later he would hand me money for it. I went through the process of losing a lot of weight, and he handed me money to buy clothes that fit or whatever workout equipment I wanted, and I did not have to ask for it.

The other day, I was downstairs exercising with my resistance bands. He was upstairs resting—he had just put in a sixteen-hour day. My band broke, and I was afraid the sound of it might have disturbed him—I thought he was sleeping. Five minutes later, he came downstairs and left the house before I could ask where he was going. When he came home, he had three new resistance bands for me. God showed me favor again.

I have been with my husband for sixteen years now, and I have never had to walk to or from the parking lot when we go out. He has always dropped me off at the door and then parked the car. He has opened every door, including the car door, for sixteen years. He shows me the utmost respect at all times. He has never raised his voice to me. He has never called me a name, or taken an angry tone, or raised a hand. He has shown unconditional love to my children. He has never said one unkind word about my family or anyone else. He is a good friend to me and my family. He is a great provider and protector. And he freely gives affection that I want or need, no matter how long his day has been. What more could I want?

I see how God has rewarded me for my faithfulness to him. God shows me favor all the time. When we are "in the fire," we just don't see it—we are too busy going through the junk in our own minds to see all the favorable things that God has done for us. God shows me favor all the time, and my husband was that way for sixteen years. Now, suddenly, I'm awake. Thank you, Jesus, and I'm sorry I didn't notice sooner.

CHAPTER 11

Rise to His Priesthood

I was stumped, wondering what I could write to help you understand clearly what we, as women, need to do to help our husbands rise to their priesthood.

I'll return to personal experience, as always. When it comes to my husband, I usually wonder how I can make his day better, so when he comes home or goes to his very burdensome job, he can function at his best. When I become the wife he needs, then and only then can he become all God wants him to be in his priesthood.

The definition of priesthood is,

"The state, order, or office of a priest; the power and authority of God." It is through the power of priesthood that God's plan of salvation is brought to pass. Our role in this as wives is very critical, and if we interfere in this, our husbands will never become who they are supposed to become in God. I had to be obedient and quiet. When I say "quiet," I mean that I had to choose my words carefully and make sure that they were always positive, kind, and supportive. I asked him constantly, "Is there anything I can do for you? Is there something I can get for you to eat or drink?".This would let him know that I was there for him.

This type of behavior gives a man the feeling of being royalty. I know if I walked in the door of my home every day, and someone wanted to serve me and wait on me and asked me if there was something he could do for me, I would feel very important. In truth, I wouldn't know how to respond. Would you? How important would that make you feel?

I have seen, through this type of action from me, that God has moved in my husband's life so much. He has a strong sense of power. He has the freedom to be in charge over all aspects of his life. He knows how to provide for his family and knows what's best for them. He can handle the finances, keep his family safe, knows his role as leader of the home, and knows without doubt that he is in charge. He does all of this with love and compassion and a firmness about him that clearly says, "That's my final decision." It is very important here that as a wife, I do not argue.

If I don't agree with something, I just go to God and complain but never to my husband. By doing this faithfully, God moves—sometimes not the way I think he should, but I do trust God and my husband. Both know what is best for me.

This works! I lived this and still am living it, and God will raise my husband up to a priesthood in the home and in a far better way than I ever could with my complaining, disagreeing, or fighting with him. It is amazing! Who are we that we think we can do a better job than God?

Every day, every year, it is easier and easier, and now it is to the point that it takes no effort on my part to trust my husband and God. Life is effortless and carefree. I think I have peace that most people don't understand or have in their lives and homes. When I listen to women talk, the things they stress over are simply not important to me.

Just yesterday, my husband wasn't feeling well physically. We were sitting on the couch, watching TV, and he was buried in his paperwork. I asked him, "How do you feel?" He replied, "Actually, I feel better." I said, "It's because you are home, and when you are at home, you always feel better." Then I asked, "Do you think you have a good home?" He said, "I have a great home! I love it!"

My interpretation of that was that I have done a good job.

CHAPTER 12

Praise from Public

After what seemed to be years of mountain climbing for me—in the sense of learning experiences, trial and error, falling down, and getting up, only to fall down again and get back up again—the world loved my husband so much that everyone said positive things about him all the time. No one ever says anything negative about him—ever. God has shown this man so much favor in the eyes of the public and with friends and family that everybody loves him—everybody!

His bosses moved him up the corporate ladder so quickly, it seems like a dream. The highest authorities in this state totally respect him, as do all of his peers. He deserves all of their praises; he has earned it.

I try hard not to break the law when driving. I feel that it would be a stain on his career, and I don't want anyone to say to him, "Hey, I pulled your wife over for speeding." This would be shameful to him—not that he would ever write me a ticket, but it is a respect thing with me. I don't want anyone complaining to him about me.

But I have been pulled over two times. One time was because a headlight was out, and the other time was for speeding—but let me explain this. When it came to car stuff, my husband handled all of it. He just hadn't gotten around to fixing the headlight yet, and I didn't know how to fix something like that.

As for the speeding thing, we have a road near our home on which the speed limit changes from 40 mph to 50 mph to 35 mph, and if you're not paying close attention to the signs, you can get caught quickly, as the road is heavily patrolled. I was on the phone with my husband as I was driving. I usually do not talk on the phone while driving, but I had been at the doctors, and my husband called me to ask how the appointment went. I didn't realize I was in a 40 mph zone, doing 50 mph. As soon as I saw the red, white, and blue lights flashing, I knew what I had done. I handed my information to the officer, and he recognized my name. He then gave me what seemed to be a cheerleading session, singing my husband's praises, and then he let me go.

Whenever I meet anyone—and I mean anyone—who knows or has heard of my husband, every word anyone says about him is positive. Even when if they don't know him personally, they will say something like, "I have never had the honor of meeting him, but I've heard he is a great guy. Maybe someday I will meet him, if I'm lucky."

Can you imagine hearing that about your husband, every time you talk to someone? Life and death are in the power of the tongue, and all this positive talk constantly is out there about him. The power is unbelievable; there are no boundaries to how far he will go or what he will become. I would like to believe that I had a small part in his rise to success, and maybe I have. I know in my heart that whenever I spoke of him, it was always uplifting and positive ... but God did the rest. This is my reward: I have a husband of whom I can be proud, and everybody loves him and respects him. I know that for God to make a great man, he has to have people in his life who are willing to lay the groundwork.

I was willing to do all I could do, through obedience to God, for my husband. If you are a wife, please choose your words carefully. They will have a enormous effect on your life and his life. Your words truly will have life-or-death importance for you both. My husband and I are living proof of that.

CHAPTER 13

The Husband You Want

When we women get married, we are under the delusion that *this* man is the answer to all our problems. We believe that he is going to be the compassionate, caring, understanding, unconditional attentive lover of our dreams, and all will be okay. This is true. And he will be, forever. What we don't realize is that marriage is like a diamond, and a diamond is formed deep beneath the earth's surface at high temperatures and pressure.

Of course, we don't think about this as we walk down the aisle or while on our honeymoon—that life is a fairy tale; the real living starts when we get home. When the honeymoon is over, and the kids are here, and the bills pile up—mortgage, electric bills, water bills, car notes, grocery bills—or when he forgets to put down the toilet seat, and you sit down in the middle of the night and get wet, this is real life. Or when he leaves his underwear on the floor, he puts his dishes are in the sink after you just cleaned up from dinner, or his coffee cup is on the nightstand for two days because you're waiting for him to bring it down to the kitchen, this is real life. He tracks mud in the house on his shoes, or he brings in the grass after mowing the lawn, and he actually burps and farts. As soon as you sit down, he needs something. When you ask him to take out the trash, you eventually just do it yourself, because he will walk past it over and over until it starts trickling on the floor, and the dog gets in it and gets a severe case of puddle butt. You clean the bathroom and the very next day, the sink is filled with shaving stubble and toothpaste. How does this prince look now?

All women face these situations. As I said, marriage is like a diamond, but think carefully about this: a diamond is formed deep under the earth's surface, under high heat and pressure and almost always in a rock.

Does this mean my husband is a rock? Having had three husbands, I can most assuredly tell you they are as stubborn as rocks—unmovable, hard, and they most certainly move at their own pace.

But I will tell you with great joy that you are the key to your husband's being a diamond. You will need to dig deep in your soul. You will need to deal with *you*. You will feel the pressure, and you will hit a brick wall, much like rock.

The Bible tells us that when we have done all we can do, just stand! Keep your smile, get on your knees, and tell God. Do all you can for him all the time, and believe that God will bring forth a diamond for all your efforts—and he will. I guarantee it.

It never seems fair that we, as women, have to sacrifice so much. We are the ones who have to walk into the fire and do battle with the Enemy, who always tries to destroy. It's like a losing battle, but remember who won in the Bible. I imagine it was *not* easy for my Lord either.

When we, as women, become the army for our husbands—defending, sacrificing, tearing down the strongholds on our husbands by prayer—then and only then they will be the husbands we want because God will see to it. He promises.

CHAPTER 14

Heavy Is the Crown

We live in a world that promotes success, especially for women. Many books out there about women in power. The movies and TV shows about women taking control of their husbands, I believe, are the very destruction of our marriages and children. God never gave us a husband to control. When God made Eve, he made her from Adam's rib, to be beside him as support, not to rule over him. I'm not saying there is anything wrong with successful women in the workplace. I'm specifically talking about a man and wife here.

The man of the house has to answer before God about so many things. Why would you want that job? He solely is responsible for leading by example, teaching the children how to act, spiritual growth, salvation, food on the table, finances, a roof over heads, safety, and being a husband, father, and friend. He also has to work enough to pay for all of this. I see what my husband goes through, and I clearly do not want that job.

Don't we, as wives, have enough to do—raising children, cooking, cleaning, taking the kids to extra activities, and just the daily mess around the house. It's enough to make anyone tired! With all we have to think about, why in the world would we want to take on more by wanting control of our husbands? We can't get control anyway—it was never God's design, so it will never happen. If you control your husband, the marriage will not be blessed, and there will not be peace in your house. You will have taken on an overload that you are not equipped to deal with—never were, never intended!

God gave men different responsibilities from women, because men can deal with things in an unemotional way. We women are way too emotional to handle everything.

There likely is chaos in your home—the balance is all out of whack, right? You are stressed out and freaking out because you suddenly have to deal with the chores, kids, pets, cooking, laundry, a job, and finances and managing your husband. If that isn't bad enough, there might be house problems or car situations, if a car breaks down. Now *you* have the weight of the spiritual responsibility for the entire family. If this is you, I have to ask, how is your sleeping? It surely cannot be peaceful or replenishing. I would think that no matter how much rest you get, it's never be enough.

You, my friend, are running on overload. And your brain never shuts down long enough to rest.

Let your husband be the man. Give it to him, give it to God, but don't take this all on yourself. You can't do it. Why would you want to do that?

There is nothing wrong with admitting we need help. It does not make us any less of a woman. We are not any weaker as a person. I believe that asking for help makes me a wiser person. I have peace. I sleep well. I go about my day thinking only of things that concern me. All else is his problem.

When I let my husband be in control of me and all that comes with me and around me, I just sit back and enjoy the ride. When you do the same, God will put your house in order, no matter what's going on. The burden is his. Just take care of the people in the house and the house. Give him the mess of everything to deal with, even if you think he can't. He will; God will make him do it. Believe that. Women are the keepers of the homes. How is your home? Is it peaceful? Or is everything in a constant state of rushed panic, and nothing ever seems to be finished or quiet?

Breathe! Take this very minute and tell the only Man who has ever loved you unconditionally and died for you that you need help. Let him wrap his arms around you. Fall asleep in his arms.

Trust me; he will deal with everything. It's not your responsibility. Throw in the towel, because you have had enough! His peace will be with you. He promised! And your home will be in order.

CHAPTER 15

All Falls into Place

These are some powerful words: all falls into place. Once I got over myself and my arrogant, self-centered, disobedient, argumentative, disagreeing ways, life was so much easier, so lighter, and so much simpler.

Everything fell into place. Now, I'm the richest woman in the world. I have it all. I have a husband who loves me more now than I could ever have dreamed was possible. He is successful, respected, loved by everyone, in charge of all his affairs as a husband, and great provider. My home is in order, my children are in the kingdom, but most important, there is peace in my home, and God is in charge.

I employ you to be a servant. Be obedient to the voice of God. Get over your insecurities of needing to have control, and ask yourself, "What do I really control any way?" Is it just in your mind? Is it only that you think you control situations? You don't.

"I am the Alpha and Omega, the beginning and the end" (Revelation 22:13). God is the only one in control, the only one who ever was. All of our insignificant, tireless efforts to do things our way are in vain. They also take too much of our energy and time—time that could be spent on much more important things in life, such as love and our families.

"For he gives his angels [especial] charge over you to accompany and defend and preserve you in all your ways [of obedience and service]" (Psalm 91:11).

"For just as by one man's disobedience [failing to hear, heedlessness and carelessness] the many were constituted sinners, so by one man's obedience the many will be constituted righteous [made acceptable to God, brought into right standing with him]" (Romans 5:19).

"Do you not know that if you continually surrender yourselves to anyone to do his will, you are the slaves of him whom you obey, whether that be to sin, which leads to death, or to obedience which leads to righteousness [right doing and right standing with God]?" (Romans 6:16).

"A woman should learn in quietness and full submission" (1 Timothy 2:11).

This is the only way to be blessed in our homes and lives, the only true happiness, the only true peace. When we do this as wives, we will have all the riches of a woman blessed by God. God will bring all things to order in our homes and husbands and lives. To live any other way is useless. There will be no fruit from all our hard work. All will be for nothing. Where's the honor in that?

I do not want my life to be for nothing. I want to see progress for all I have learned through my pain. I want blessings on my children, home, husband, finances, and everything else. If I do not have this, what is the point of my existence or of my marriage?

I guess it all comes down to whether or not we want life at all. I do. What about you?